# Landon's Local Government

I0799197

Jon Wiles

Infomax Readers

Rosen Classroom™

New York

Published in 2014 by The Rosen Publishing Group, Inc.
29 East 21st Street, New York, NY 10010



Book Design: Katelyn Londino

Photo Credits: Cover (city hall) Aaron Kohr/Shutterstock.com; cover (boy) serrnovik/Shutterstock.com; pp. 3–24 (border) Bagiuiani/Shutterstock.com; p. 5 Thomas Barrat/Shutterstock.com; p. 7 Stephen Coburn/Shutterstock.com; p. 9 Jetta Productions/Iconica/Getty Images; p. 11 Mike Flippo/Shutterstock.com; p. 13 Ernest R. Prim/Shutterstock.com; p. 15 (main) Goodluz/Shutterstock.com; p. 15 (top inset) vadim kozlovsky/Shutterstock.com; p. 15 (bottom inset) hans.slegers/Shutterstock.com; p. 17 David Livingston/Getty Images Entertainment/Getty Images; p. 19 Jack Hollingsworth/Thinkstock.com; p. 21 (traffic light) ktsdesign/Shutterstock.com; p. 21 (crossing guard) Lisa F. Young/Shutterstock.com; p. 21 (library) qushe/Shutterstock.com; p. 21 (park) cheng/Shutterstock.com; p. 22 antpkr/Shutterstock.com.

ISBN: 978-1-4777-2634-1
6-pack ISBN: 978-1-4777-2635-8

Manufactured in the United States of America

CPSIA Compliance Information: Batch #CS13RC: For further information contact Rosen Publishing, New York, New York at 1-800-237-9932.

# Contents

# Field Trip

Landon is going on a field trip to city hall! That's the big brick building in his town where the local government meets to work on city business.

Landon's teacher, Mrs. Sanchez, says that local government is very important to the everyday lives of its citizens. It takes care of the things people want and need, such as public parks, schools, and construction. Local government also **determines** the laws and finances of the city.

Hopefully, by learning about local government, Landon will understand more about how his community works.

# What Is Local Government?

First, Landon wants to learn what local government means. As they enter city hall, Mrs. Sanchez says there are three major kinds of government: national, state, and local.

National government, also called federal government, takes care of the laws and big decisions that affect everyone in the country. State government takes care of laws and decisions for the state only. Local government is special because it takes care of the laws and decisions for smaller communities, like counties, cities, towns, or villages.

There's a big room in Landon's city hall where important people meet and make decisions about local government.

Mrs. Sanchez teaches Landon's class about the people who work in local government. Each city governs itself a bit differently from others. In many communities, the head of the local government is the mayor. The mayor has a **council** that helps him make decisions and take care of city business.

Usually the council meets at least once a month to talk about city matters. Any community member can go to these meetings and get involved in local government.

Sometimes Landon's mom goes to city council meetings so she can stay updated on city business.

One of the major **responsibilities** of local government is making local laws. National governments make many important laws for the country, and states make laws, too. However, people in a town or city must also follow the laws set by local government.

For example, in Landon's city, people can't make too much noise after 11:00 p.m. There are also speed limits and laws telling people where they can park. These local laws are important because they match the needs of the community.

Another local law in Landon's town is that dogs aren't allowed to run loose. This makes the community safer for people and for dogs!

# City Projects

Collecting taxes from citizens is another important responsibility of local government. Citizens pay taxes on things they buy and land they own. Local government uses tax money to pay for public services all citizens need.

Taxes **fund** public works, or construction projects that take care of roads and buildings. Landon sees a construction crew fixing the road outside city hall. They're making the road safer to travel on. They're also fixing the traffic lights so people can drive safely.

The public works department also checks buildings to make sure they're safe places to live and work.

Landon thinks his community is a nice place to live. It's very clean, and that's because the public works department helps to keep it that way. Trash collectors work for the public works department. Their job is to remove all the trash that people leave out.

The public works department cleans up water when there's a flood. They also remove leaves from the streets in the fall. That way, the streets are clean.

At city hall, Landon gets to meet a worker from the public works department!

# Keeping People Safe

Taxes also pay for **emergency** services, like the police department. Police officers are very important because they **enforce** laws. They work to keep people from mistreating animals, property, and other people.

Taxes also fund Landon's local fire department. Firefighters help prevent fires from happening by checking buildings for fire risks. They also put out fires and save people and animals from being hurt.

Police officers and firefighters sometimes visit Landon's school to teach students about living safely.

OWENS

# School, Books, and Fun!

Landon learns that his local government pays for things all kids need, such as education. Public schools are funded by tax money. That makes it possible for all kids to learn from teachers, books, and computers at school.

Landon loves books. There's a huge library right next to city hall, which is also funded by tax money. He borrows many kinds of books so he can learn something new every day!

Mrs. Sanchez teaches at a public school, so the local government pays her to educate her students!

Landon's favorite thing offered by his local government is **recreation**. The parks department in city hall takes care of the parks and fun activities to do in his city. That way, everyone can exercise and have fun outside!

Landon likes to play baseball at the park near his house. In the summer, there are arts and crafts at the park, too. Sometimes there are special events for the community, such as the summer fair!

# Public Services

## What Does Tax Money Fund?

| public works projects | public safety | education | recreation |
| --- | --- | --- | --- |
| trash collection | police officers | schools | community events |
| roadwork | firefighters | teachers | sports |
| traffic lights | crossing guards | libraries | parks |

# Getting Involved

Landon had a great field trip to city hall. He even met a city council member! She told his class it's important for kids to get involved in their local government.

To get involved, kids can write letters about issues important to them. Also, they can return to city hall for council meetings to learn more about important events in the city. Landon thinks the best thing about local government is that all citizens can get involved!

# Glossary

**council** (KOWN-suhl) A group of people chosen to make laws for a community.

**determine** (dih-TUHR-muhn) To decide finally and without question.

**emergency** (ih-MUHR-juhn-see) A serious event that needs immediate action.

**enforce** (ihn-FOHRS) To make people obey.

**fund** (FUHND) To pay for.

**recreation** (reh-kree-AY-shun) An activity that is relaxing and fun.

**responsibility** (rih-spahn-suh-BIH-luh-tee) A duty.

# Index